My Garden Journal

Brenda J. Sullivan

This Journal Belongs to

_____

_____

My Garden Journal
By Brenda J. Sullivan

© 2020 All Rights Reserved Brenda J. Sullivan, Thompson Street Farm LLC

Artwork by Kathryn A. Sullivan and Brenda J. Sullivan

No part of this book may be reproduced or transmitted in any form or by any means, mechanical or electronic, including photocopying or recording, or by an information storage and retrieval systems, or transmitted by email without permission in writing from the publisher.

ISBN: 978-1-7329990-5-3

Photographs/Illustrations:
Brenda J. Sullivan
Kathryn A. Sullivan
Google Images
Pixabay
Creative Commons
Nate Solberg - Scout Collective

To learn more about our books or join our newsletter go to
www.brendajsullivanbooks.com
brenda@brendajsullivanbooks.com

Published by Tree Roots Press
Requests to publish work from this book should be sent to:
treerootspress@gmail.com

www.treerootspress.com

To my sweet Katie - I love you!

Me cutting lavender in the garden

Introduction

Congratulations on your interest in learning how to garden! Whether it's in a yard, a community garden plot, a porch, or in a sunny room in your house, the purpose of this book is to help you get started.

This journal shares years of my gardening experience in all kinds of weather, spaces, and containers here in my town. In my opinion, keeping a journal is the only way to improve one's skills. After years of trial and error, I finally figured out what worked and what didn't by creating my own garden journal.

The following growing season I could review my past journals and repeat my successes. My garden logs also helped me avoid making the same previous mistakes from the growing seasons. In gardening it's essential to know what works and what doesn't.

Several years ago, I was asked to develop a curriculum for a farm to school program and my gardening journal pages were the perfect outline for the syllabus. After tweaking a few sections, the journal pages in this book are the final result of these fantastic, student experiences.

This book is not meant to be a complete how-to garden book, but a place to begin. Gardening is a journey that never ends as long as you continue to grow something.

In the resource section, I've included some of my favorite gardening websites and books. As you get more experienced, you will want to move on to more advanced techniques.

Good luck and happy gardening!

Sincerely,
Brenda J. Sullivan
Thompson Street Farm LLC
Farm to Bath

Picture of Plant

Year _____

Plant: _____

Grown in: _____

Container: _____ Raised Bed: _____

Ground: _____

Planted Where?

Full Sun: _____ Shade: _____

Part Sun /Part Shade: _____

Did I start this plant from seed? _____

Date started seedlings: _____

Date I direct seeded: _____

I bought this plant: _____

Date planted: _____

How many planted: _____

Date harvested: _____

What was my yield for this plant(s)?

_____

Growing Notes
Suggested questions: How well did this plant grow? Any problem(s) growing this plant? If so, how did I fix it?
How often did I have to water and was it enough?

Harvesting Notes

Suggested questions: What did the product look like? Did I grow too much or too little? Was there enough product to feed me? What was the color, smell, taste? Did I like it? Did it meet my expectations?

Plant

_____

_____

Soil Amendments Used

Before Planting: _____ During Growing Season: _____

After Harvesting: _____

(i.e. commercial compost; homemade compost; worm castings; compost tea)

What type of soil did this plant grow in?   Loam: _____   Clay Soil: _____

        Commercial Potting Soil: _____   Sandy Loam: _____   Don't know: _____

I purchased this seed or plant from: _____

Was it Organic?: _____ or Non-organic?: _____

What was my purpose for growing this plant? _____

_____

What parts of the plant did I eat (if edible)? *(e.g. root, leaf, fruit, flower)*: _____

_____

If I didn't eat the plant, what did I do with it? *(e.g. made flower bouquets or I liked growing it for fun)*:

_____

Would I grow this plant again? If not why?

Picture of Plant

Year _____

Plant: _____

Grown in: _____

Container: _____ Raised Bed: _____

Ground: _____

Planted Where?

Full Sun: _____ Shade: _____

Part Sun /Part Shade: _____

Did I start this plant from seed? _____

Date started seedlings: _____

Date I direct seeded: _____

I bought this plant: _____

Date planted: _____

How many planted: _____

Date harvested: _____

What was my yield for this plant(s)?

_____

Growing Notes
Suggested questions: How well did this plant grow? Any problem(s) growing this plant? If so, how did I fix it? How often did I have to water and was it enough?

My Garden Journal

Harvesting Notes

Suggested questions: What did the product look like? Did I grow too much or too little? Was there enough product to feed me? What was the color, smell, taste? Did I like it? Did it meet my expectations?

Plant

_____

_____

Soil Amendments Used

Before Planting: _____ During Growing Season: _____

After Harvesting: _____

(i.e. commercial compost; homemade compost; worm castings; compost tea)

What type of soil did this plant grow in?   Loam: _____   Clay Soil: _____

    Commercial Potting Soil: _____   Sandy Loam: _____   Don't know: _____

I purchased this seed or plant from: _____

Was it Organic?: _____ or Non-organic?: _____

What was my purpose for growing this plant? _____

_____

What parts of the plant did I eat (if edible)? *(e.g. root, leaf, fruit, flower)*: _____

_____

If I didn't eat the plant, what did I do with it? *(e.g. made flower bouquets or I liked growing it for fun)*:

_____

Would I grow this plant again? If not why?

© 2020 All Rights Reserved Brenda J. Sullivan, Thompson Street Farm LLC

Picture of Plant

Year _____

Plant: _____

Grown in: _____

Container: _____ Raised Bed: _____

Ground: _____

Planted Where?

Full Sun: _____ Shade: _____

Part Sun /Part Shade: _____

Did I start this plant from seed? _____

Date started seedlings: _____

Date I direct seeded: _____

I bought this plant: _____

Date planted: _____

How many planted: _____

Date harvested: _____

What was my yield for this plant(s)?

_____

Growing Notes

Suggested questions: How well did this plant grow? Any problem(s) growing this plant? If so, how did I fix it? How often did I have to water and was it enough?

My Garden Journal

Harvesting Notes

Suggested questions: What did the product look like? Did I grow too much or too little? Was there enough product to feed me? What was the color, smell, taste? Did I like it? Did it meet my expectations?

Plant

_____

Soil Amendments Used

Before Planting: _____ During Growing Season: _____

After Harvesting: _____

(i.e. commercial compost; homemade compost; worm castings; compost tea)

What type of soil did this plant grow in? Loam: _____ Clay Soil: _____

Commercial Potting Soil: _____ Sandy Loam: _____ Don't know: _____

I purchased this seed or plant from: _____

Was it Organic?: _____ or Non-organic?: _____

What was my purpose for growing this plant? _____

_____

What parts of the plant did I eat (if edible)? *(e.g. root, leaf, fruit, flower)*: _____

_____

If I didn't eat the plant, what did I do with it? *(e.g. made flower bouquets or I liked growing it for fun)*:

_____

Would I grow this plant again? If not why?

My Garden Journal

Picture of Plant

Year _____

Plant: _____

Grown in: _____

Container: _____ Raised Bed: _____

Ground: _____

Planted Where?

Full Sun: _____ Shade: _____

Part Sun /Part Shade: _____

Did I start this plant from seed? _____

Date started seedlings: _____

Date I direct seeded: _____

I bought this plant: _____

Date planted: _____

How many planted: _____

Date harvested: _____

What was my yield for this plant(s)?

_____

Growing Notes
Suggested questions: How well did this plant grow? Any problem(s) growing this plant? If so, how did I fix it? How often did I have to water and was it enough?

© 2020 All Rights Reserved Brenda J. Sullivan, Thompson Street Farm LLC

My Garden Journal

Harvesting Notes

Suggested questions: What did the product look like? Did I grow too much or too little? Was there enough product to feed me? What was the color, smell, taste? Did I like it? Did it meet my expectations?

Plant

_____

_____

Soil Amendments Used

Before Planting: _____ During Growing Season: _____

After Harvesting: _____
(i.e. commercial compost; homemade compost; worm castings; compost tea)

What type of soil did this plant grow in?   Loam: _____   Clay Soil: _____

    Commercial Potting Soil: _____   Sandy Loam: _____   Don't know: _____

I purchased this seed or plant from: _____

                                            Was it Organic?: _____ or Non-organic?: _____

What was my purpose for growing this plant? _____

_____

What parts of the plant did I eat (if edible)? *(e.g. root, leaf, fruit, flower)*: _____

_____

If I didn't eat the plant, what did I do with it? *(e.g. made flower bouquets or I liked growing it for fun)*:

_____

Would I grow this plant again? If not why?

© 2020 All Rights Reserved Brenda J. Sullivan, Thompson Street Farm LLC

Picture of Plant

Year _____

Plant: _____

Grown in: _____

Container: _____ Raised Bed: _____

Ground: _____

Planted Where?

Full Sun: _____ Shade: _____

Part Sun /Part Shade: _____

Did I start this plant from seed? _____

Date started seedlings: _____

Date I direct seeded: _____

I bought this plant: _____

Date planted: _____

How many planted: _____

Date harvested: _____

What was my yield for this plant(s)?

_____

Growing Notes
Suggested questions: How well did this plant grow? Any problem(s) growing this plant? If so, how did I fix it?
How often did I have to water and was it enough?

Harvesting Notes

Suggested questions: What did the product look like? Did I grow too much or too little? Was there enough product to feed me? What was the color, smell, taste? Did I like it? Did it meet my expectations?

Plant
_____

Soil Amendments Used

Before Planting: _____ During Growing Season: _____

After Harvesting: _____

(i.e. commercial compost; homemade compost; worm castings; compost tea)

What type of soil did this plant grow in?   Loam: _____   Clay Soil: _____

Commercial Potting Soil: _____   Sandy Loam: _____   Don't know: _____

I purchased this seed or plant from: _____

Was it Organic?: _____ or Non-organic?: _____

What was my purpose for growing this plant? _____

_____

What parts of the plant did I eat (if edible)? *(e.g. root, leaf, fruit, flower)*: _____

_____

If I didn't eat the plant, what did I do with it? *(e.g. made flower bouquets or I liked growing it for fun)*:

_____

Would I grow this plant again? If not why?

Picture of Plant

Year _____

Plant: _____

Grown in: _____

Container: _____ Raised Bed: _____

Ground: _____

Planted Where?

Full Sun: _____ Shade: _____

Part Sun /Part Shade: _____

Did I start this plant from seed? _____

Date started seedlings: _____

Date I direct seeded: _____

I bought this plant: _____

Date planted: _____

How many planted: _____

Date harvested: _____

What was my yield for this plant(s)?

_____

Growing Notes
Suggested questions: How well did this plant grow? Any problem(s) growing this plant? If so, how did I fix it? How often did I have to water and was it enough?

Harvesting Notes

Suggested questions: What did the product look like? Did I grow too much or too little? Was there enough product to feed me? What was the color, smell, taste? Did I like it? Did it meet my expectations?

Plant

_____

Soil Amendments Used

Before Planting: _____ During Growing Season: _____

After Harvesting: _____
(i.e. commercial compost; homemade compost; worm castings; compost tea)

What type of soil did this plant grow in? Loam: _____ Clay Soil: _____

    Commercial Potting Soil: _____ Sandy Loam: _____ Don't know: _____

I purchased this seed or plant from: _____

    Was it Organic?: _____ or Non-organic?: _____

What was my purpose for growing this plant? _____

_____

What parts of the plant did I eat (if edible)? *(e.g. root, leaf, fruit, flower):* _____

_____

If I didn't eat the plant, what did I do with it? *(e.g. made flower bouquets or I liked growing it for fun):*

_____

Would I grow this plant again? If not why?

My Garden Journal

Picture of Plant

Year _____

Plant: _____

Grown in: _____

Container: _____ Raised Bed: _____

Ground: _____

Planted Where?

Full Sun: _____ Shade: _____

Part Sun /Part Shade: _____

Did I start this plant from seed? _____

Date started seedlings: _____

Date I direct seeded: _____

I bought this plant: _____

Date planted: _____

How many planted: _____

Date harvested: _____

What was my yield for this plant(s)?

_____

Growing Notes

Suggested questions: How well did this plant grow? Any problem(s) growing this plant? If so, how did I fix it? How often did I have to water and was it enough?

My Garden Journal

Harvesting Notes

Suggested questions: What did the product look like? Did I grow too much or too little? Was there enough product to feed me? What was the color, smell, taste? Did I like it? Did it meet my expectations?

Plant

_____

Soil Amendments Used

Before Planting: _____ During Growing Season: _____

After Harvesting: _____

(i.e. commercial compost; homemade compost; worm castings; compost tea)

What type of soil did this plant grow in?   Loam: _____   Clay Soil: _____

Commercial Potting Soil: _____   Sandy Loam: _____   Don't know: _____

I purchased this seed or plant from: _____

Was it Organic?: _____ or Non-organic?: _____

What was my purpose for growing this plant? _____

_____

What parts of the plant did I eat (if edible)? *(e.g. root, leaf, fruit, flower):* _____

_____

If I didn't eat the plant, what did I do with it? *(e.g. made flower bouquets or I liked growing it for fun):*

_____

Would I grow this plant again? If not why?

© 2020 All Rights Reserved Brenda J. Sullivan, Thompson Street Farm LLC

My Garden Journal

Picture of Plant | **Year** _____

Plant: _____

Grown in: _____

Container: _____ Raised Bed: _____

Ground: _____

Planted Where?

Full Sun: _____ Shade: _____

Part Sun /Part Shade: _____

Did I start this plant from seed? _____

Date started seedlings: _____

Date I direct seeded: _____

I bought this plant: _____

Date planted: _____

How many planted: _____

Date harvested: _____

What was my yield for this plant(s)?

_____

Growing Notes
Suggested questions: How well did this plant grow? Any problem(s) growing this plant? If so, how did I fix it? How often did I have to water and was it enough?

© 2020 All Rights Reserved Brenda J. Sullivan, Thompson Street Farm LLC

My Garden Journal

Harvesting Notes

Suggested questions: What did the product look like? Did I grow too much or too little? Was there enough product to feed me? What was the color, smell, taste? Did I like it? Did it meet my expectations?

Plant

_____

_____

Soil Amendments Used

Before Planting: _____ During Growing Season: _____

After Harvesting: _____

(i.e. commercial compost; homemade compost; worm castings; compost tea)

What type of soil did this plant grow in?   Loam: _____   Clay Soil: _____

       Commercial Potting Soil: _____   Sandy Loam: _____   Don't know: _____

I purchased this seed or plant from: _____

                                        Was it Organic?: _____ or Non-organic?: _____

What was my purpose for growing this plant? _____

_____

What parts of the plant did I eat (if edible)? *(e.g. root, leaf, fruit, flower):* _____

_____

If I didn't eat the plant, what did I do with it? *(e.g. made flower bouquets or I liked growing it for fun):*

_____

Would I grow this plant again? If not why?

My Garden Journal

Picture of Plant

Year _____

Plant: _____

Grown in: _____

Container: _____ Raised Bed: _____

Ground: _____

Planted Where?

Full Sun: _____ Shade: _____

Part Sun /Part Shade: _____

Did I start this plant from seed? _____

Date started seedlings: _____

Date I direct seeded: _____

I bought this plant: _____

Date planted: _____

How many planted: _____

Date harvested: _____

What was my yield for this plant(s)?

_____

Growing Notes
Suggested questions: How well did this plant grow? Any problem(s) growing this plant? If so, how did I fix it? How often did I have to water and was it enough?

My Garden Journal

Harvesting Notes

Suggested questions: What did the product look like? Did I grow too much or too little? Was there enough product to feed me? What was the color, smell, taste? Did I like it? Did it meet my expectations?

Plant

_____

_____

Soil Amendments Used

Before Planting: _____ During Growing Season: _____

After Harvesting: _____
(i.e. commercial compost; homemade compost; worm castings; compost tea)

What type of soil did this plant grow in?　　　　　　　Loam: _____　　　Clay Soil: _____

　　　　Commercial Potting Soil: _____　　Sandy Loam: _____　　Don't know: _____

I purchased this seed or plant from: _____

　　　　　　　　　　　　　　　　　　Was it Organic?: _____ or Non-organic?: _____

What was my purpose for growing this plant? _____

_____

What parts of the plant did I eat (if edible)? *(e.g. root, leaf, fruit, flower):* _____

_____

If I didn't eat the plant, what did I do with it? *(e.g. made flower bouquets or I liked growing it for fun):*
_____

Would I grow this plant again? If not why?

© 2020 All Rights Reserved Brenda J. Sullivan, Thompson Street Farm LLC

My Garden Journal

Picture of Plant | **Year** _____

Plant: _____

Grown in: _____

Container: _____ Raised Bed: _____

Ground: _____

Planted Where?

Full Sun: _____ Shade: _____

Part Sun /Part Shade: _____

Did I start this plant from seed? _____

Date started seedlings: _____

Date I direct seeded: _____

I bought this plant: _____

Date planted: _____

How many planted: _____

Date harvested: _____

What was my yield for this plant(s)?

_____

Growing Notes
Suggested questions: How well did this plant grow? Any problem(s) growing this plant? If so, how did I fix it? How often did I have to water and was it enough?

© 2020 All Rights Reserved Brenda J. Sullivan, Thompson Street Farm LLC

Harvesting Notes

Suggested questions: What did the product look like? Did I grow too much or too little? Was there enough product to feed me? What was the color, smell, taste? Did I like it? Did it meet my expectations?

Plant

_____

_____

Soil Amendments Used

Before Planting: _____ During Growing Season: _____

After Harvesting: _____
(i.e. commercial compost; homemade compost; worm castings; compost tea)

What type of soil did this plant grow in?   Loam: _____   Clay Soil: _____

      Commercial Potting Soil: _____   Sandy Loam: _____   Don't know: _____

I purchased this seed or plant from: _____

Was it Organic?: _____ or Non-organic?: _____

What was my purpose for growing this plant? _____
_____

What parts of the plant did I eat (if edible)? *(e.g. root, leaf, fruit, flower):* _____
_____

If I didn't eat the plant, what did I do with it? *(e.g. made flower bouquets or I liked growing it for fun):*
_____

Would I grow this plant again? If not why?

Picture of Plant

Year _____

Plant: _____

Grown in: _____

Container: _____ Raised Bed: _____

Ground: _____

Planted Where?

Full Sun: _____ Shade: _____

Part Sun /Part Shade: _____

Did I start this plant from seed? _____

Date started seedlings: _____

Date I direct seeded: _____

I bought this plant: _____

Date planted: _____

How many planted: _____

Date harvested: _____

What was my yield for this plant(s)?

_____

Growing Notes
Suggested questions: How well did this plant grow? Any problem(s) growing this plant? If so, how did I fix it?
How often did I have to water and was it enough?

My Garden Journal

Harvesting Notes

Suggested questions: What did the product look like? Did I grow too much or too little? Was there enough product to feed me? What was the color, smell, taste? Did I like it? Did it meet my expectations?

Plant

_____

_____

Soil Amendments Used

Before Planting: _____ During Growing Season: _____

After Harvesting: _____

(i.e. commercial compost; homemade compost; worm castings; compost tea)

What type of soil did this plant grow in?   Loam: _____   Clay Soil: _____

        Commercial Potting Soil: _____   Sandy Loam: _____   Don't know: _____

I purchased this seed or plant from: _____

                                            Was it Organic?: _____ or Non-organic?: _____

What was my purpose for growing this plant? _____

_____

What parts of the plant did I eat (if edible)? *(e.g. root, leaf, fruit, flower):* _____

_____

If I didn't eat the plant, what did I do with it? *(e.g. made flower bouquets or I liked growing it for fun):*

_____

Would I grow this plant again? If not why?

My Garden Journal

Picture of Plant

Year _____

Plant: _____

Grown in: _____

Container: _____ Raised Bed: _____

Ground: _____

Planted Where?

Full Sun: _____ Shade: _____

Part Sun /Part Shade: _____

Did I start this plant from seed? _____

Date started seedlings: _____

Date I direct seeded: _____

I bought this plant: _____

Date planted: _____

How many planted: _____

Date harvested: _____

What was my yield for this plant(s)?

_____

Growing Notes
Suggested questions: How well did this plant grow? Any problem(s) growing this plant? If so, how did I fix it? How often did I have to water and was it enough?

© 2020 All Rights Reserved Brenda J. Sullivan, Thompson Street Farm LLC

Harvesting Notes

Suggested questions: What did the product look like? Did I grow too much or too little? Was there enough product to feed me? What was the color, smell, taste? Did I like it? Did it meet my expectations?

Plant

_____

_____

Soil Amendments Used

Before Planting: _____ During Growing Season: _____

After Harvesting: _____
(i.e. commercial compost; homemade compost; worm castings; compost tea)

What type of soil did this plant grow in?   Loam: _____   Clay Soil: _____

    Commercial Potting Soil: _____   Sandy Loam: _____   Don't know: _____

I purchased this seed or plant from: _____

                                    Was it Organic?: _____ or Non-organic?: _____

What was my purpose for growing this plant? _____

_____

What parts of the plant did I eat (if edible)? *(e.g. root, leaf, fruit, flower):* _____

_____

If I didn't eat the plant, what did I do with it? *(e.g. made flower bouquets or I liked growing it for fun):*

_____

Would I grow this plant again? If not why?

My Garden Journal

Picture of Plant

Year _____

Plant: _____

Grown in: _____

Container: _____ Raised Bed: _____

Ground: _____

Planted Where?

Full Sun: _____ Shade: _____

Part Sun /Part Shade: _____

Did I start this plant from seed? _____

Date started seedlings: _____

Date I direct seeded: _____

I bought this plant: _____

Date planted: _____

How many planted: _____

Date harvested: _____

What was my yield for this plant(s)?

_____

Growing Notes

Suggested questions: How well did this plant grow? Any problem(s) growing this plant? If so, how did I fix it? How often did I have to water and was it enough?

My Garden Journal

Harvesting Notes

Suggested questions: What did the product look like? Did I grow too much or too little? Was there enough product to feed me? What was the color, smell, taste? Did I like it? Did it meet my expectations?

Plant

_____

_____

Soil Amendments Used

Before Planting: _____ During Growing Season: _____

After Harvesting: _____

(i.e. commercial compost; homemade compost; worm castings; compost tea)

What type of soil did this plant grow in?   Loam: _____   Clay Soil: _____

    Commercial Potting Soil: _____   Sandy Loam: _____   Don't know: _____

I purchased this seed or plant from: _____

                                                 Was it Organic?: _____ or Non-organic?: _____

What was my purpose for growing this plant? _____

_____

What parts of the plant did I eat (if edible)? *(e.g. root, leaf, fruit, flower):* _____

_____

If I didn't eat the plant, what did I do with it? *(e.g. made flower bouquets or I liked growing it for fun):*

_____

Would I grow this plant again? If not why?

© 2020 All Rights Reserved Brenda J. Sullivan, Thompson Street Farm LLC

Picture of Plant

Year _____

Plant: _____

Grown in: _____

Container: _____ Raised Bed: _____

Ground: _____

Planted Where?

Full Sun: _____ Shade: _____

Part Sun /Part Shade: _____

Did I start this plant from seed? _____

Date started seedlings: _____

Date I direct seeded: _____

I bought this plant: _____

Date planted: _____

How many planted: _____

Date harvested: _____

What was my yield for this plant(s)?

_____

Growing Notes
Suggested questions: How well did this plant grow? Any problem(s) growing this plant? If so, how did I fix it? How often did I have to water and was it enough?

Harvesting Notes

Suggested questions: What did the product look like? Did I grow too much or too little? Was there enough product to feed me? What was the color, smell, taste? Did I like it? Did it meet my expectations?

Plant

_____

_____

Soil Amendments Used

Before Planting: _____ During Growing Season: _____

After Harvesting: _____

(i.e. commercial compost; homemade compost; worm castings; compost tea)

What type of soil did this plant grow in?   Loam: _____   Clay Soil: _____

    Commercial Potting Soil: _____   Sandy Loam: _____   Don't know: _____

I purchased this seed or plant from: _____

    Was it Organic?: _____ or Non-organic?: _____

What was my purpose for growing this plant? _____

_____

What parts of the plant did I eat (if edible)? *(e.g. root, leaf, fruit, flower):* _____

_____

If I didn't eat the plant, what did I do with it? *(e.g. made flower bouquets or I liked growing it for fun):*

_____

Would I grow this plant again? If not why?

Picture of Plant

Year _____

Plant: _____

Grown in: _____

Container: _____ Raised Bed: _____

Ground: _____

Planted Where?

Full Sun: _____ Shade: _____

Part Sun /Part Shade: _____

Did I start this plant from seed? _____

Date started seedlings: _____

Date I direct seeded: _____

I bought this plant: _____

Date planted: _____

How many planted: _____

Date harvested: _____

What was my yield for this plant(s)?

_____

Growing Notes

Suggested questions: How well did this plant grow? Any problem(s) growing this plant? If so, how did I fix it?
How often did I have to water and was it enough?

My Garden Journal

Harvesting Notes

Suggested questions: What did the product look like? Did I grow too much or too little? Was there enough product to feed me? What was the color, smell, taste? Did I like it? Did it meet my expectations?

Plant

_____

_____

Soil Amendments Used

Before Planting: _____ During Growing Season: _____

After Harvesting:_____

(i.e. commercial compost; homemade compost; worm castings; compost tea)

What type of soil did this plant grow in?   Loam: _____   Clay Soil: _____

        Commercial Potting Soil: _____   Sandy Loam: _____   Don't know: _____

I purchased this seed or plant from: _____

Was it Organic?: _____ or Non-organic?: _____

What was my purpose for growing this plant? _____

_____

What parts of the plant did I eat (if edible)? *(e.g. root, leaf, fruit, flower)*: _____

_____

If I didn't eat the plant, what did I do with it? *(e.g. made flower bouquets or I liked growing it for fun)*:

_____

Would I grow this plant again? If not why?

© 2020 All Rights Reserved Brenda J. Sullivan, Thompson Street Farm LLC

My Garden Journal

Picture of Plant | **Year** _____

Plant: _____

Grown in: _____

Container: _____ Raised Bed: _____

Ground: _____

Planted Where?

Full Sun: _____ Shade: _____

Part Sun /Part Shade: _____

Did I start this plant from seed? _____

Date started seedlings: _____

Date I direct seeded: _____

I bought this plant: _____

Date planted: _____

How many planted: _____

Date harvested: _____

What was my yield for this plant(s)?

_____

Growing Notes
Suggested questions: How well did this plant grow? Any problem(s) growing this plant? If so, how did I fix it? How often did I have to water and was it enough?

Harvesting Notes

Suggested questions: What did the product look like? Did I grow too much or too little? Was there enough product to feed me? What was the color, smell, taste? Did I like it? Did it meet my expectations?

Plant

_____

Soil Amendments Used

Before Planting: _____ During Growing Season: _____

After Harvesting: _____
(i.e. commercial compost; homemade compost; worm castings; compost tea)

What type of soil did this plant grow in?   Loam: _____   Clay Soil: _____

     Commercial Potting Soil: _____   Sandy Loam: _____   Don't know: _____

I purchased this seed or plant from: _____

Was it Organic?: _____ or Non-organic?: _____

What was my purpose for growing this plant? _____

_____

What parts of the plant did I eat (if edible)? *(e.g. root, leaf, fruit, flower):* _____

_____

If I didn't eat the plant, what did I do with it? *(e.g. made flower bouquets or I liked growing it for fun):*

_____

Would I grow this plant again? If not why?

© 2020 All Rights Reserved Brenda J. Sullivan, Thompson Street Farm LLC

Picture of Plant

My Garden Journal

Year _____

Plant: _____

Grown in: _____

Container: _____ Raised Bed: _____

Ground: _____

Planted Where?

Full Sun: _____ Shade: _____

Part Sun /Part Shade: _____

Did I start this plant from seed? _____

Date started seedlings: _____

Date I direct seeded: _____

I bought this plant: _____

Date planted: _____

How many planted: _____

Date harvested: _____

What was my yield for this plant(s)?

_____

Growing Notes
Suggested questions: How well did this plant grow? Any problem(s) growing this plant? If so, how did I fix it? How often did I have to water and was it enough?

My Garden Journal

Harvesting Notes

Suggested questions: What did the product look like? Did I grow too much or too little? Was there enough product to feed me? What was the color, smell, taste? Did I like it? Did it meet my expectations?

Plant

_____

Soil Amendments Used

Before Planting: _____ During Growing Season: _____

After Harvesting: _____

(i.e. commercial compost; homemade compost; worm castings; compost tea)

What type of soil did this plant grow in?   Loam: _____   Clay Soil: _____

    Commercial Potting Soil: _____   Sandy Loam: _____   Don't know: _____

I purchased this seed or plant from: _____

                                   Was it Organic?: _____ or Non-organic?: _____

What was my purpose for growing this plant? _____

_____

What parts of the plant did I eat (if edible)? *(e.g. root, leaf, fruit, flower):* _____

_____

If I didn't eat the plant, what did I do with it? *(e.g. made flower bouquets or I liked growing it for fun):*

_____

Would I grow this plant again? If not why?

© 2020 All Rights Reserved Brenda J. Sullivan, Thompson Street Farm LLC

My Garden Journal

Picture of Plant | **Year**_____

Plant: _____

Grown in: _____

Container: _____ Raised Bed: _____

Ground: _____

Planted Where?

Full Sun: _____ Shade: _____

Part Sun /Part Shade: _____

Did I start this plant from seed?_____

Date started seedlings: _____

Date I direct seeded: _____

I bought this plant: _____

Date planted: _____

How many planted: _____

Date harvested: _____

What was my yield for this plant(s)?

_____

Growing Notes
Suggested questions: How well did this plant grow? Any problem(s) growing this plant? If so, how did I fix it? How often did I have to water and was it enough?

© 2020 All Rights Reserved Brenda J. Sullivan, Thompson Street Farm LLC

Harvesting Notes

Suggested questions: What did the product look like? Did I grow too much or too little? Was there enough product to feed me? What was the color, smell, taste? Did I like it? Did it meet my expectations?

Plant
_____

_____

Soil Amendments Used

Before Planting: _____ During Growing Season: _____

After Harvesting: _____
(i.e. commercial compost; homemade compost; worm castings; compost tea)

What type of soil did this plant grow in?   Loam: _____   Clay Soil: _____

    Commercial Potting Soil: _____   Sandy Loam: _____   Don't know: _____

I purchased this seed or plant from: _____

                                      Was it Organic?: _____ or Non-organic?: _____

What was my purpose for growing this plant? _____

_____

What parts of the plant did I eat (if edible)? *(e.g. root, leaf, fruit, flower):* _____

_____

If I didn't eat the plant, what did I do with it? *(e.g. made flower bouquets or I liked growing it for fun):*

_____

Would I grow this plant again? If not why?

Picture of Plant

Year _____

Plant: _____

Grown in: _____

Container: _____ Raised Bed: _____

Ground: _____

Planted Where?

Full Sun: _____ Shade: _____

Part Sun /Part Shade: _____

Did I start this plant from seed? _____

Date started seedlings: _____

Date I direct seeded: _____

I bought this plant: _____

Date planted: _____

How many planted: _____

Date harvested: _____

What was my yield for this plant(s)?

_____

Growing Notes
Suggested questions: How well did this plant grow? Any problem(s) growing this plant? If so, how did I fix it? How often did I have to water and was it enough?

My Garden Journal

Harvesting Notes

Suggested questions: What did the product look like? Did I grow too much or too little? Was there enough product to feed me? What was the color, smell, taste? Did I like it? Did it meet my expectations?

Plant

_____

Soil Amendments Used

Before Planting: _____ During Growing Season: _____

After Harvesting: _____
(i.e. commercial compost; homemade compost; worm castings; compost tea)

What type of soil did this plant grow in?   Loam: _____   Clay Soil: _____

      Commercial Potting Soil: _____   Sandy Loam: _____   Don't know: _____

I purchased this seed or plant from: _____

      Was it Organic?: _____ or Non-organic?: _____

What was my purpose for growing this plant? _____

_____

What parts of the plant did I eat (if edible)? *(e.g. root, leaf, fruit, flower)*: _____

_____

If I didn't eat the plant, what did I do with it? *(e.g. made flower bouquets or I liked growing it for fun)*:

_____

Would I grow this plant again? If not why?

Picture of Plant | **Year** _____

Plant: _____

Grown in: _____

Container: _____ Raised Bed: _____

Ground: _____

Planted Where?

Full Sun: _____ Shade: _____

Part Sun /Part Shade: _____

Did I start this plant from seed? _____

Date started seedlings: _____

Date I direct seeded: _____

I bought this plant: _____

Date planted: _____

How many planted: _____

Date harvested: _____

What was my yield for this plant(s)?

_____

Growing Notes
Suggested questions: How well did this plant grow? Any problem(s) growing this plant? If so, how did I fix it? How often did I have to water and was it enough?

My Garden Journal

Harvesting Notes

Suggested questions: What did the product look like? Did I grow too much or too little? Was there enough product to feed me? What was the color, smell, taste? Did I like it? Did it meet my expectations?

Plant

_____

_____

Soil Amendments Used

Before Planting: _____ During Growing Season: _____

After Harvesting:_____
(i.e. commercial compost; homemade compost; worm castings; compost tea)

What type of soil did this plant grow in?   Loam: _____   Clay Soil: _____

        Commercial Potting Soil: _____   Sandy Loam: _____   Don't know: _____

I purchased this seed or plant from: _____

        Was it Organic?: _____ or Non-organic?: _____

What was my purpose for growing this plant? _____

_____

What parts of the plant did I eat (if edible)? *(e.g. root, leaf, fruit, flower):* _____

_____

If I didn't eat the plant, what did I do with it? *(e.g. made flower bouquets or I liked growing it for fun):*

_____

Would I grow this plant again? If not why?

Picture of Plant

Year _____

Plant: _____

Grown in: _____

Container: _____ Raised Bed: _____

Ground: _____

Planted Where?

Full Sun: _____ Shade: _____

Part Sun /Part Shade: _____

Did I start this plant from seed? _____

Date started seedlings: _____

Date I direct seeded: _____

I bought this plant: _____

Date planted: _____

How many planted: _____

Date harvested: _____

What was my yield for this plant(s)?

_____

Growing Notes

Suggested questions: How well did this plant grow? Any problem(s) growing this plant? If so, how did I fix it? How often did I have to water and was it enough?

My Garden Journal

Harvesting Notes

Suggested questions: What did the product look like? Did I grow too much or too little? Was there enough product to feed me? What was the color, smell, taste? Did I like it? Did it meet my expectations?

Plant

_____

_____

Soil Amendments Used

Before Planting: _____ During Growing Season: _____

After Harvesting: _____
(i.e. commercial compost; homemade compost; worm castings; compost tea)

What type of soil did this plant grow in? Loam: _____ Clay Soil: _____

Commercial Potting Soil: _____ Sandy Loam: _____ Don't know: _____

I purchased this seed or plant from: _____

Was it Organic?: _____ or Non-organic?: _____

What was my purpose for growing this plant? _____

_____

What parts of the plant did I eat (if edible)? *(e.g. root, leaf, fruit, flower):* _____

_____

If I didn't eat the plant, what did I do with it? *(e.g. made flower bouquets or I liked growing it for fun):*

_____

Would I grow this plant again? If not why?

Picture of Plant

Year _____

Plant: _____

Grown in: _____

Container: _____ Raised Bed: _____

Ground: _____

Planted Where?

Full Sun: _____ Shade: _____

Part Sun /Part Shade: _____

Did I start this plant from seed? _____

Date started seedlings: _____

Date I direct seeded: _____

I bought this plant: _____

Date planted: _____

How many planted: _____

Date harvested: _____

What was my yield for this plant(s)?

_____

Growing Notes
Suggested questions: How well did this plant grow? Any problem(s) growing this plant? If so, how did I fix it? How often did I have to water and was it enough?

Harvesting Notes

Suggested questions: What did the product look like? Did I grow too much or too little? Was there enough product to feed me? What was the color, smell, taste? Did I like it? Did it meet my expectations?

Plant

_____

_____

Soil Amendments Used

Before Planting: _____ During Growing Season: _____

After Harvesting: _____
(i.e. commercial compost; homemade compost; worm castings; compost tea)

What type of soil did this plant grow in?　　　　　　　　　Loam: _____　　　Clay Soil: _____

　　　　　Commercial Potting Soil: _____　　Sandy Loam: _____　　Don't know: _____

I purchased this seed or plant from: _____

　　　　　　　　　　　　　　　　　　Was it Organic?: _____ or Non-organic?: _____

What was my purpose for growing this plant? _____

_____

What parts of the plant did I eat (if edible)? *(e.g. root, leaf, fruit, flower):* _____

_____

If I didn't eat the plant, what did I do with it? *(e.g. made flower bouquets or I liked growing it for fun):*

_____

Would I grow this plant again? If not why?

Picture of Plant

Year _____

Plant: _____

Grown in: _____

Container: _____ Raised Bed: _____

Ground: _____

Planted Where?

Full Sun: _____ Shade: _____

Part Sun /Part Shade: _____

Did I start this plant from seed? _____

Date started seedlings: _____

Date I direct seeded: _____

I bought this plant: _____

Date planted: _____

How many planted: _____

Date harvested: _____

What was my yield for this plant(s)?

_____

Growing Notes
Suggested questions: How well did this plant grow? Any problem(s) growing this plant? If so, how did I fix it? How often did I have to water and was it enough?

Harvesting Notes

Suggested questions: What did the product look like? Did I grow too much or too little? Was there enough product to feed me? What was the color, smell, taste? Did I like it? Did it meet my expectations?

Plant

_____

_____

Soil Amendments Used

Before Planting: _____ During Growing Season: _____

After Harvesting: _____
(i.e. commercial compost; homemade compost; worm castings; compost tea)

What type of soil did this plant grow in?   Loam: _____   Clay Soil: _____

        Commercial Potting Soil: _____   Sandy Loam: _____   Don't know: _____

I purchased this seed or plant from: _____

                                              Was it Organic?: _____ or Non-organic?: _____

What was my purpose for growing this plant? _____

_____

What parts of the plant did I eat (if edible)? *(e.g. root, leaf, fruit, flower)*: _____

_____

If I didn't eat the plant, what did I do with it? *(e.g. made flower bouquets or I liked growing it for fun)*:

_____

Would I grow this plant again? If not why?

© 2020 All Rights Reserved Brenda J. Sullivan, Thompson Street Farm LLC

Picture of Plant

Year _____

Plant: _____

Grown in: _____

Container: _____ Raised Bed: _____

Ground: _____

Planted Where?

Full Sun: _____ Shade: _____

Part Sun /Part Shade: _____

Did I start this plant from seed? _____

Date started seedlings: _____

Date I direct seeded: _____

I bought this plant: _____

Date planted: _____

How many planted: _____

Date harvested: _____

What was my yield for this plant(s)?

_____

Growing Notes

Suggested questions: How well did this plant grow? Any problem(s) growing this plant? If so, how did I fix it? How often did I have to water and was it enough?

Harvesting Notes

Suggested questions: What did the product look like? Did I grow too much or too little? Was there enough product to feed me? What was the color, smell, taste? Did I like it? Did it meet my expectations?

Plant

_____

_____

Soil Amendments Used

Before Planting: _____ During Growing Season: _____

After Harvesting: _____

(i.e. commercial compost; homemade compost; worm castings; compost tea)

What type of soil did this plant grow in?   Loam: _____   Clay Soil: _____

        Commercial Potting Soil: _____   Sandy Loam: _____   Don't know: _____

I purchased this seed or plant from: _____

Was it Organic?: _____ or Non-organic?: _____

What was my purpose for growing this plant? _____

_____

What parts of the plant did I eat (if edible)? *(e.g. root, leaf, fruit, flower):* _____

_____

If I didn't eat the plant, what did I do with it? *(e.g. made flower bouquets or I liked growing it for fun):*

_____

Would I grow this plant again? If not why?

My Garden Journal

Picture of Plant | **Year**_____

Plant: _____

Grown in:_____

Container: _____ Raised Bed: _____

Ground: _____

Planted Where?

Full Sun: _____ Shade: _____

Part Sun /Part Shade: _____

Did I start this plant from seed?_____

Date started seedlings: _____

Date I direct seeded: _____

I bought this plant: _____

Date planted: _____

How many planted: _____

Date harvested: _____

What was my yield for this plant(s)?

_____

Growing Notes
Suggested questions: How well did this plant grow? Any problem(s) growing this plant? If so, how did I fix it?
How often did I have to water and was it enough?

© 2020 All Rights Reserved Brenda J. Sullivan, Thompson Street Farm LLC

Harvesting Notes

Suggested questions: What did the product look like? Did I grow too much or too little? Was there enough product to feed me? What was the color, smell, taste? Did I like it? Did it meet my expectations?

Plant

_____

_____

Soil Amendments Used

Before Planting: _____ During Growing Season: _____

After Harvesting:_____

(i.e. commercial compost; homemade compost; worm castings; compost tea)

What type of soil did this plant grow in?   Loam: _____   Clay Soil: _____

    Commercial Potting Soil: _____   Sandy Loam: _____   Don't know: _____

I purchased this seed or plant from: _____

Was it Organic?: _____ or Non-organic?: _____

What was my purpose for growing this plant? _____

_____

What parts of the plant did I eat (if edible)? *(e.g. root, leaf, fruit, flower):* _____

_____

If I didn't eat the plant, what did I do with it? *(e.g. made flower bouquets or I liked growing it for fun):*

_____

Would I grow this plant again? If not why?

Picture of Plant

My Garden Journal

Year _____

Plant: _____

Grown in: _____

Container: _____ Raised Bed: _____

Ground: _____

Planted Where?

Full Sun: _____ Shade: _____

Part Sun /Part Shade: _____

Did I start this plant from seed? _____

Date started seedlings: _____

Date I direct seeded: _____

I bought this plant: _____

Date planted: _____

How many planted: _____

Date harvested: _____

What was my yield for this plant(s)?

_____

Growing Notes
Suggested questions: How well did this plant grow? Any problem(s) growing this plant? If so, how did I fix it? How often did I have to water and was it enough?

My Garden Journal

Harvesting Notes

Suggested questions: What did the product look like? Did I grow too much or too little? Was there enough product to feed me? What was the color, smell, taste? Did I like it? Did it meet my expectations?

Plant _____
_____

Soil Amendments Used

Before Planting: _____ During Growing Season: _____

After Harvesting: _____
(i.e. commercial compost; homemade compost; worm castings; compost tea)

What type of soil did this plant grow in?   Loam: _____   Clay Soil: _____

    Commercial Potting Soil: _____   Sandy Loam: _____   Don't know: _____

I purchased this seed or plant from: _____

    Was it Organic?: _____ or Non-organic?: _____

What was my purpose for growing this plant? _____

_____

What parts of the plant did I eat (if edible)? *(e.g. root, leaf, fruit, flower):* _____

_____

If I didn't eat the plant, what did I do with it? *(e.g. made flower bouquets or I liked growing it for fun):*

_____

Would I grow this plant again? If not why?

My Garden Journal

Picture of Plant

Year_____

Plant: _____

Grown in:_____

Container: _____ Raised Bed: _____

Ground:_____

Planted Where?

Full Sun: _____ Shade: _____

Part Sun /Part Shade: _____

Did I start this plant from seed?_____

Date started seedlings: _____

Date I direct seeded: _____

I bought this plant: _____

Date planted: _____

How many planted: _____

Date harvested: _____

What was my yield for this plant(s)?

_____

Growing Notes
Suggested questions: How well did this plant grow? Any problem(s) growing this plant? If so, how did I fix it? How often did I have to water and was it enough?

© 2020 All Rights Reserved Brenda J. Sullivan, Thompson Street Farm LLC

Harvesting Notes

Suggested questions: What did the product look like? Did I grow too much or too little? Was there enough product to feed me? What was the color, smell, taste? Did I like it? Did it meet my expectations?

Plant
_____

_____

Soil Amendments Used

Before Planting: _____ During Growing Season: _____

After Harvesting:_____
(i.e. commercial compost; homemade compost; worm castings; compost tea)

What type of soil did this plant grow in?　　　　　　　　Loam: _____　　　　Clay Soil: _____

　　　　　　Commercial Potting Soil: _____　　Sandy Loam: _____　　　Don't know: _____

I purchased this seed or plant from: _____

　　　　　　　　　　　　　　　　　　　　　Was it Organic?: _____ or Non-organic?: _____

What was my purpose for growing this plant? _____

_____

What parts of the plant did I eat (if edible)? *(e.g. root, leaf, fruit, flower)*: _____

_____

If I didn't eat the plant, what did I do with it? *(e.g. made flower bouquets or I liked growing it for fun)*:

_____

Would I grow this plant again? If not why?

© 2020 All Rights Reserved Brenda J. Sullivan, Thompson Street Farm LLC

My Garden Journal

Picture of Plant | **Year** _____

Plant: _____

Grown in: _____

Container: _____ Raised Bed: _____

Ground: _____

Planted Where?

Full Sun: _____ Shade: _____

Part Sun /Part Shade: _____

Did I start this plant from seed? _____

Date started seedlings: _____

Date I direct seeded: _____

I bought this plant: _____

Date planted: _____

How many planted: _____

Date harvested: _____

What was my yield for this plant(s)?

_____

Growing Notes
Suggested questions: How well did this plant grow? Any problem(s) growing this plant? If so, how did I fix it? How often did I have to water and was it enough?

My Garden Journal

Harvesting Notes

Suggested questions: What did the product look like? Did I grow too much or too little? Was there enough product to feed me? What was the color, smell, taste? Did I like it? Did it meet my expectations?

Plant

_____

_____

Soil Amendments Used

Before Planting: _____ During Growing Season: _____

After Harvesting: _____
(i.e. commercial compost; homemade compost; worm castings; compost tea)

What type of soil did this plant grow in?   Loam: _____   Clay Soil: _____

    Commercial Potting Soil: _____   Sandy Loam: _____   Don't know: _____

I purchased this seed or plant from: _____

    Was it Organic?: _____ or Non-organic?: _____

What was my purpose for growing this plant? _____

_____

What parts of the plant did I eat (if edible)? *(e.g. root, leaf, fruit, flower)*: _____

_____

If I didn't eat the plant, what did I do with it? *(e.g. made flower bouquets or I liked growing it for fun)*:

_____

Would I grow this plant again? If not why?

© 2020 All Rights Reserved Brenda J. Sullivan, Thompson Street Farm LLC

My Garden Journal

Picture of Plant

Year _____

Plant: _____

Grown in: _____

Container: _____ Raised Bed: _____

Ground: _____

Planted Where?

Full Sun: _____ Shade: _____

Part Sun /Part Shade: _____

Did I start this plant from seed? _____

Date started seedlings: _____

Date I direct seeded: _____

I bought this plant: _____

Date planted: _____

How many planted: _____

Date harvested: _____

What was my yield for this plant(s)?

_____

Growing Notes
Suggested questions: How well did this plant grow? Any problem(s) growing this plant? If so, how did I fix it? How often did I have to water and was it enough?

My Garden Journal

Harsh... **Harvesting Notes**

Suggested questions: What did the product look like? Did I grow too much or too little? Was there enough product to feed me? What was the color, smell, taste? Did I like it? Did it meet my expectations?

Plant

_____

Soil Amendments Used

Before Planting: _____ During Growing Season: _____

After Harvesting: _____

(i.e. commercial compost; homemade compost; worm castings; compost tea)

What type of soil did this plant grow in? Loam: _____ Clay Soil: _____

Commercial Potting Soil: _____ Sandy Loam: _____ Don't know: _____

I purchased this seed or plant from: _____

Was it Organic?: _____ or Non-organic?: _____

What was my purpose for growing this plant? _____

_____

What parts of the plant did I eat (if edible)? *(e.g. root, leaf, fruit, flower):* _____

_____

If I didn't eat the plant, what did I do with it? *(e.g. made flower bouquets or I liked growing it for fun):*

_____

Would I grow this plant again? If not why?

Picture of Plant

My Garden Journal

Year _____

Plant: _____

Grown in: _____

Container: _____ Raised Bed: _____

Ground: _____

Planted Where?

Full Sun: _____ Shade: _____

Part Sun /Part Shade: _____

Did I start this plant from seed? _____

Date started seedlings: _____

Date I direct seeded: _____

I bought this plant: _____

Date planted: _____

How many planted: _____

Date harvested: _____

What was my yield for this plant(s)?

_____

Growing Notes
Suggested questions: How well did this plant grow? Any problem(s) growing this plant? If so, how did I fix it? How often did I have to water and was it enough?

My Garden Journal

Harvesting Notes

Suggested questions: What did the product look like? Did I grow too much or too little? Was there enough product to feed me? What was the color, smell, taste? Did I like it? Did it meet my expectations?

Plant

_____

_____

Soil Amendments Used

Before Planting: _____ During Growing Season: _____

After Harvesting: _____

(i.e. commercial compost; homemade compost; worm castings; compost tea)

What type of soil did this plant grow in?   Loam: _____   Clay Soil: _____

    Commercial Potting Soil: _____   Sandy Loam: _____   Don't know: _____

I purchased this seed or plant from: _____

                                            Was it Organic?: _____ or Non-organic?: _____

What was my purpose for growing this plant? _____

_____

What parts of the plant did I eat (if edible)? *(e.g. root, leaf, fruit, flower)*: _____

_____

If I didn't eat the plant, what did I do with it? *(e.g. made flower bouquets or I liked growing it for fun)*:

_____

Would I grow this plant again? If not why?

© 2020 All Rights Reserved Brenda J. Sullivan, Thompson Street Farm LLC

Picture of Plant

My Garden Journal

Year _____

Plant: _____

Grown in: _____

Container: _____ Raised Bed: _____

Ground: _____

Planted Where?

Full Sun: _____ Shade: _____

Part Sun /Part Shade: _____

Did I start this plant from seed? _____

Date started seedlings: _____

Date I direct seeded: _____

I bought this plant: _____

Date planted: _____

How many planted: _____

Date harvested: _____

What was my yield for this plant(s)?

_____

Growing Notes
Suggested questions: How well did this plant grow? Any problem(s) growing this plant? If so, how did I fix it? How often did I have to water and was it enough?

© 2020 All Rights Reserved Brenda J. Sullivan, Thompson Street Farm LLC

Harvesting Notes

Suggested questions: What did the product look like? Did I grow too much or too little? Was there enough product to feed me? What was the color, smell, taste? Did I like it? Did it meet my expectations?

Plant

_____

_____

Soil Amendments Used

Before Planting: _____ During Growing Season: _____

After Harvesting: _____

(i.e. commercial compost; homemade compost; worm castings; compost tea)

What type of soil did this plant grow in?   Loam: _____   Clay Soil: _____

    Commercial Potting Soil: _____   Sandy Loam: _____   Don't know: _____

I purchased this seed or plant from: _____

                                                           Was it Organic?: _____ or Non-organic?: _____

What was my purpose for growing this plant? _____

_____

What parts of the plant did I eat (if edible)? *(e.g. root, leaf, fruit, flower)*: _____

_____

If I didn't eat the plant, what did I do with it? *(e.g. made flower bouquets or I liked growing it for fun)*:

_____

Would I grow this plant again? If not why?

My Garden Journal

Picture of Plant | **Year** _____

Plant: _____

Grown in: _____

Container: _____ Raised Bed: _____

Ground: _____

Planted Where?

Full Sun: _____ Shade: _____

Part Sun /Part Shade: _____

Did I start this plant from seed? _____

Date started seedlings: _____

Date I direct seeded: _____

I bought this plant: _____

Date planted: _____

How many planted: _____

Date harvested: _____

What was my yield for this plant(s)?

_____

Growing Notes
Suggested questions: How well did this plant grow? Any problem(s) growing this plant? If so, how did I fix it? How often did I have to water and was it enough?

© 2020 All Rights Reserved Brenda J. Sullivan, Thompson Street Farm LLC

My Garden Journal

Harvesting Notes

Suggested questions: What did the product look like? Did I grow too much or too little? Was there enough product to feed me? What was the color, smell, taste? Did I like it? Did it meet my expectations?

Plant

_____

_____

Soil Amendments Used

Before Planting: _____   During Growing Season: _____

After Harvesting: _____

(i.e. commercial compost; homemade compost; worm castings; compost tea)

What type of soil did this plant grow in?   Loam: _____   Clay Soil: _____

Commercial Potting Soil: _____   Sandy Loam: _____   Don't know: _____

I purchased this seed or plant from: _____

Was it Organic?: _____ or Non-organic?: _____

What was my purpose for growing this plant? _____

_____

What parts of the plant did I eat (if edible)? *(e.g. root, leaf, fruit, flower):* _____

_____

If I didn't eat the plant, what did I do with it? *(e.g. made flower bouquets or I liked growing it for fun):*

_____

Would I grow this plant again? If not why?

My Garden Journal

Picture of Plant

Year _____

Plant: _____

Grown in: _____

Container: _____ Raised Bed: _____

Ground: _____

Planted Where?

Full Sun: _____ Shade: _____

Part Sun /Part Shade: _____

Did I start this plant from seed? _____

Date started seedlings: _____

Date I direct seeded: _____

I bought this plant: _____

Date planted: _____

How many planted: _____

Date harvested: _____

What was my yield for this plant(s)?

_____

Growing Notes
Suggested questions: How well did this plant grow? Any problem(s) growing this plant? If so, how did I fix it? How often did I have to water and was it enough?

Harvesting Notes

Suggested questions: What did the product look like? Did I grow too much or too little? Was there enough product to feed me? What was the color, smell, taste? Did I like it? Did it meet my expectations?

Plant

_____

_____

Soil Amendments Used

Before Planting: _____ During Growing Season: _____

After Harvesting: _____

(i.e. commercial compost; homemade compost; worm castings; compost tea)

What type of soil did this plant grow in?　　　　　　　Loam: _____　　　　Clay Soil: _____

　　　　Commercial Potting Soil: _____　　Sandy Loam: _____　　Don't know: _____

I purchased this seed or plant from: _____

　　　　　　　　　　　　　　　　　　Was it Organic?: _____ or Non-organic?: _____

What was my purpose for growing this plant? _____

_____

What parts of the plant did I eat (if edible)? *(e.g. root, leaf, fruit, flower):* _____

_____

If I didn't eat the plant, what did I do with it? *(e.g. made flower bouquets or I liked growing it for fun):*

_____

Would I grow this plant again? If not why?

Picture of Plant

Year _____

Plant: _____

Grown in: _____

Container: _____ Raised Bed: _____

Ground: _____

Planted Where?

Full Sun: _____ Shade: _____

Part Sun /Part Shade: _____

Did I start this plant from seed? _____

Date started seedlings: _____

Date I direct seeded: _____

I bought this plant: _____

Date planted: _____

How many planted: _____

Date harvested: _____

What was my yield for this plant(s)?

_____

Growing Notes
Suggested questions: How well did this plant grow? Any problem(s) growing this plant? If so, how did I fix it? How often did I have to water and was it enough?

Harvesting Notes

Suggested questions: What did the product look like? Did I grow too much or too little? Was there enough product to feed me? What was the color, smell, taste? Did I like it? Did it meet my expectations?

Plant

_____

_____

Soil Amendments Used

Before Planting: _____ During Growing Season: _____

After Harvesting: _____
(i.e. commercial compost; homemade compost; worm castings; compost tea)

What type of soil did this plant grow in?   Loam: _____   Clay Soil: _____

    Commercial Potting Soil: _____   Sandy Loam: _____   Don't know: _____

I purchased this seed or plant from: _____

    Was it Organic?: _____   or Non-organic?: _____

What was my purpose for growing this plant? _____

_____

What parts of the plant did I eat (if edible)? *(e.g. root, leaf, fruit, flower):* _____

_____

If I didn't eat the plant, what did I do with it? *(e.g. made flower bouquets or I liked growing it for fun):*

_____

Would I grow this plant again? If not why?

My Garden Journal

Picture of Plant

Year _____

Plant: _____

Grown in: _____

Container: _____ Raised Bed: _____

Ground: _____

Planted Where?

Full Sun: _____ Shade: _____

Part Sun /Part Shade: _____

Did I start this plant from seed? _____

Date started seedlings: _____

Date I direct seeded: _____

I bought this plant: _____

Date planted: _____

How many planted: _____

Date harvested: _____

What was my yield for this plant(s)?

_____

Growing Notes
Suggested questions: How well did this plant grow? Any problem(s) growing this plant? If so, how did I fix it? How often did I have to water and was it enough?

Harvesting Notes

Suggested questions: What did the product look like? Did I grow too much or too little? Was there enough product to feed me? What was the color, smell, taste? Did I like it? Did it meet my expectations?

Plant

_____

_____

Soil Amendments Used

Before Planting: _____ During Growing Season: _____

After Harvesting: _____

(i.e. commercial compost; homemade compost; worm castings; compost tea)

What type of soil did this plant grow in?   Loam: _____   Clay Soil: _____

    Commercial Potting Soil: _____   Sandy Loam: _____   Don't know: _____

I purchased this seed or plant from: _____

                                                          Was it Organic?: _____ or Non-organic?:_____

What was my purpose for growing this plant? _____

_____

What parts of the plant did I eat (if edible)? *(e.g. root, leaf, fruit, flower):* _____

_____

If I didn't eat the plant, what did I do with it? *(e.g. made flower bouquets or I liked growing it for fun):*

_____

Would I grow this plant again? If not why?

© 2020 All Rights Reserved Brenda J. Sullivan, Thompson Street Farm LLC

Picture of Plant

Year _____

Plant: _____

Grown in: _____

Container: _____ Raised Bed: _____

Ground: _____

Planted Where?

Full Sun: _____ Shade: _____

Part Sun /Part Shade: _____

Did I start this plant from seed? _____

Date started seedlings: _____

Date I direct seeded: _____

I bought this plant: _____

Date planted: _____

How many planted: _____

Date harvested: _____

What was my yield for this plant(s)?

_____

Growing Notes
Suggested questions: How well did this plant grow? Any problem(s) growing this plant? If so, how did I fix it? How often did I have to water and was it enough?

Harvesting Notes

Suggested questions: What did the product look like? Did I grow too much or too little? Was there enough product to feed me? What was the color, smell, taste? Did I like it? Did it meet my expectations?

Plant

_____

_____

Soil Amendments Used

Before Planting: _____ During Growing Season: _____

After Harvesting:_____
(i.e. commercial compost; homemade compost; worm castings; compost tea)

What type of soil did this plant grow in?   Loam: _____   Clay Soil: _____

    Commercial Potting Soil: _____   Sandy Loam: _____   Don't know: _____

I purchased this seed or plant from: _____

Was it Organic?: _____ or Non-organic?: _____

What was my purpose for growing this plant? _____

_____

What parts of the plant did I eat (if edible)? *(e.g. root, leaf, fruit, flower):* _____

_____

If I didn't eat the plant, what did I do with it? *(e.g. made flower bouquets or I liked growing it for fun):*

_____

Would I grow this plant again? If not why?

My Garden Journal

Picture of Plant

Year _____

Plant: _____

Grown in: _____

Container: _____ Raised Bed: _____

Ground: _____

Planted Where?

Full Sun: _____ Shade: _____

Part Sun /Part Shade: _____

Did I start this plant from seed? _____

Date started seedlings: _____

Date I direct seeded: _____

I bought this plant: _____

Date planted: _____

How many planted: _____

Date harvested: _____

What was my yield for this plant(s)?

_____

Growing Notes
Suggested questions: How well did this plant grow? Any problem(s) growing this plant? If so, how did I fix it? How often did I have to water and was it enough?

© 2020 All Rights Reserved Brenda J. Sullivan, Thompson Street Farm LLC

Harvesting Notes

Suggested questions: What did the product look like? Did I grow too much or too little? Was there enough product to feed me? What was the color, smell, taste? Did I like it? Did it meet my expectations?

Plant _____

Soil Amendments Used

Before Planting: _____ During Growing Season: _____

After Harvesting: _____

(i.e. commercial compost; homemade compost; worm castings; compost tea)

What type of soil did this plant grow in?   Loam: _____   Clay Soil: _____

Commercial Potting Soil: _____   Sandy Loam: _____   Don't know: _____

I purchased this seed or plant from: _____

Was it Organic?: _____ or Non-organic?: _____

What was my purpose for growing this plant? _____

_____

What parts of the plant did I eat (if edible)? *(e.g. root, leaf, fruit, flower)*: _____

_____

If I didn't eat the plant, what did I do with it? *(e.g. made flower bouquets or I liked growing it for fun)*:

_____

Would I grow this plant again? If not why?

My Garden Journal

Picture of Plant

Year _____

Plant: _____

Grown in: _____

Container: _____ Raised Bed: _____

Ground: _____

Planted Where?

Full Sun: _____ Shade: _____

Part Sun /Part Shade: _____

Did I start this plant from seed? _____

Date started seedlings: _____

Date I direct seeded: _____

I bought this plant: _____

Date planted: _____

How many planted: _____

Date harvested: _____

What was my yield for this plant(s)?

_____

_____

Growing Notes
Suggested questions: How well did this plant grow? Any problem(s) growing this plant? If so, how did I fix it? How often did I have to water and was it enough?

© 2020 All Rights Reserved Brenda J. Sullivan, Thompson Street Farm LLC

Harvesting Notes

Suggested questions: What did the product look like? Did I grow too much or too little? Was there enough product to feed me? What was the color, smell, taste? Did I like it? Did it meet my expectations?

Plant

_____

_____

Soil Amendments Used

Before Planting: _____ During Growing Season: _____

After Harvesting: _____
(i.e. commercial compost; homemade compost; worm castings; compost tea)

What type of soil did this plant grow in?   Loam: _____   Clay Soil: _____

    Commercial Potting Soil: _____   Sandy Loam: _____   Don't know: _____

I purchased this seed or plant from: _____

                                             Was it Organic?: _____ or Non-organic?: _____

What was my purpose for growing this plant? _____

_____

What parts of the plant did I eat (if edible)? *(e.g. root, leaf, fruit, flower)*: _____

_____

If I didn't eat the plant, what did I do with it? *(e.g. made flower bouquets or I liked growing it for fun)*:

_____

Would I grow this plant again? If not why?

Picture of Plant | **Year**_____

Plant: _____

Grown in: _____

Container: _____ Raised Bed: _____

Ground: _____

Planted Where?

Full Sun: _____ Shade: _____

Part Sun / Part Shade: _____

Did I start this plant from seed? _____

Date started seedlings: _____

Date I direct seeded: _____

I bought this plant: _____

Date planted: _____

How many planted: _____

Date harvested: _____

What was my yield for this plant(s)?

_____

Growing Notes

Suggested questions: How well did this plant grow? Any problem(s) growing this plant? If so, how did I fix it? How often did I have to water and was it enough?

Harvesting Notes

Suggested questions: What did the product look like? Did I grow too much or too little? Was there enough product to feed me? What was the color, smell, taste? Did I like it? Did it meet my expectations?

Plant

_____

Soil Amendments Used

Before Planting: _____ During Growing Season: _____

After Harvesting: _____
(i.e. commercial compost; homemade compost; worm castings; compost tea)

What type of soil did this plant grow in?   Loam: _____   Clay Soil: _____

      Commercial Potting Soil: _____   Sandy Loam: _____   Don't know: _____

I purchased this seed or plant from: _____

      Was it Organic?: _____ or Non-organic?: _____

What was my purpose for growing this plant? _____

_____

What parts of the plant did I eat (if edible)? *(e.g. root, leaf, fruit, flower):* _____

_____

If I didn't eat the plant, what did I do with it? *(e.g. made flower bouquets or I liked growing it for fun):*

_____

Would I grow this plant again? If not why?

My Garden Journal

Picture of Plant

Year_____

Plant: _____

Grown in: _____

Container: _____ Raised Bed: _____

Ground: _____

Planted Where?

Full Sun: _____ Shade: _____

Part Sun /Part Shade: _____

Did I start this plant from seed? _____

Date started seedlings: _____

Date I direct seeded: _____

I bought this plant: _____

Date planted: _____

How many planted: _____

Date harvested: _____

What was my yield for this plant(s)?

_____

Growing Notes
Suggested questions: How well did this plant grow? Any problem(s) growing this plant? If so, how did I fix it? How often did I have to water and was it enough?

© 2020 All Rights Reserved Brenda J. Sullivan, Thompson Street Farm LLC

My Garden Journal

Harvesting Notes

Suggested questions: What did the product look like? Did I grow too much or too little? Was there enough product to feed me? What was the color, smell, taste? Did I like it? Did it meet my expectations?

Plant

_____

_____

Soil Amendments Used

Before Planting: _____ During Growing Season: _____

After Harvesting: _____

(i.e. commercial compost; homemade compost; worm castings; compost tea)

What type of soil did this plant grow in?   Loam: _____   Clay Soil: _____

        Commercial Potting Soil: _____   Sandy Loam: _____   Don't know: _____

I purchased this seed or plant from: _____

Was it Organic?: _____ or Non-organic?: _____

What was my purpose for growing this plant? _____

_____

What parts of the plant did I eat (if edible)? *(e.g. root, leaf, fruit, flower)*: _____

_____

If I didn't eat the plant, what did I do with it? *(e.g. made flower bouquets or I liked growing it for fun)*:

_____

Would I grow this plant again? If not why?

© 2020 All Rights Reserved Brenda J. Sullivan, Thompson Street Farm LLC

My Garden Journal

Picture of Plant

Year _____

Plant: _____

Grown in: _____

Container: _____ Raised Bed: _____

Ground: _____

Planted Where?

Full Sun: _____ Shade: _____

Part Sun /Part Shade: _____

Did I start this plant from seed? _____

Date started seedlings: _____

Date I direct seeded: _____

I bought this plant: _____

Date planted: _____

How many planted: _____

Date harvested: _____

What was my yield for this plant(s)?

_____

Growing Notes
Suggested questions: How well did this plant grow? Any problem(s) growing this plant? If so, how did I fix it? How often did I have to water and was it enough?

© 2020 All Rights Reserved Brenda J. Sullivan, Thompson Street Farm LLC

My Garden Journal

Harvesting Notes

Suggested questions: What did the product look like? Did I grow too much or too little? Was there enough product to feed me? What was the color, smell, taste? Did I like it? Did it meet my expectations?

Plant

_____

_____

Soil Amendments Used

Before Planting: _____ During Growing Season: _____

After Harvesting: _____

(i.e. commercial compost; homemade compost; worm castings; compost tea)

What type of soil did this plant grow in?   Loam: _____   Clay Soil: _____

    Commercial Potting Soil: _____   Sandy Loam: _____   Don't know: _____

I purchased this seed or plant from: _____

                                                             Was it Organic?: _____ or Non-organic?: _____

What was my purpose for growing this plant? _____

_____

What parts of the plant did I eat (if edible)? *(e.g. root, leaf, fruit, flower):* _____

_____

If I didn't eat the plant, what did I do with it? *(e.g. made flower bouquets or I liked growing it for fun):*

_____

Would I grow this plant again? If not why?

Picture of Plant

Year _____

Plant: _____

Grown in: _____

Container: _____ Raised Bed: _____

Ground: _____

Planted Where?

Full Sun: _____ Shade: _____

Part Sun /Part Shade: _____

Did I start this plant from seed? _____

Date started seedlings: _____

Date I direct seeded: _____

I bought this plant: _____

Date planted: _____

How many planted: _____

Date harvested: _____

What was my yield for this plant(s)?

_____

Growing Notes
Suggested questions: How well did this plant grow? Any problem(s) growing this plant? If so, how did I fix it? How often did I have to water and was it enough?

Harvesting Notes

Suggested questions: What did the product look like? Did I grow too much or too little? Was there enough product to feed me? What was the color, smell, taste? Did I like it? Did it meet my expectations?

Plant

_____

_____

Soil Amendments Used

Before Planting: _____ During Growing Season: _____

After Harvesting: _____

(i.e. commercial compost; homemade compost; worm castings; compost tea)

What type of soil did this plant grow in? Loam: _____ Clay Soil: _____

Commercial Potting Soil: _____ Sandy Loam: _____ Don't know: _____

I purchased this seed or plant from: _____

Was it Organic?: _____ or Non-organic?: _____

What was my purpose for growing this plant? _____

_____

What parts of the plant did I eat (if edible)? *(e.g. root, leaf, fruit, flower)*: _____

_____

If I didn't eat the plant, what did I do with it? *(e.g. made flower bouquets or I liked growing it for fun)*:

_____

Would I grow this plant again? If not why?

Picture of Plant

My Garden Journal

Year _____

Plant: _____

Grown in: _____

Container: _____ Raised Bed: _____

Ground: _____

Planted Where?

Full Sun: _____ Shade: _____

Part Sun /Part Shade: _____

Did I start this plant from seed? _____

Date started seedlings: _____

Date I direct seeded: _____

I bought this plant: _____

Date planted: _____

How many planted: _____

Date harvested: _____

What was my yield for this plant(s)?

_____

Growing Notes
Suggested questions: How well did this plant grow? Any problem(s) growing this plant? If so, how did I fix it? How often did I have to water and was it enough?

© 2020 All Rights Reserved Brenda J. Sullivan, Thompson Street Farm LLC

My Garden Journal

Harvesting Notes

Suggested questions: What did the product look like? Did I grow too much or too little? Was there enough product to feed me? What was the color, smell, taste? Did I like it? Did it meet my expectations?

Plant
_____

Soil Amendments Used

Before Planting: _____ During Growing Season: _____

After Harvesting: _____

(i.e. commercial compost; homemade compost; worm castings; compost tea)

What type of soil did this plant grow in? Loam: _____   Clay Soil: _____

Commercial Potting Soil: _____   Sandy Loam: _____   Don't know: _____

I purchased this seed or plant from: _____

Was it Organic?: _____ or Non-organic?: _____

What was my purpose for growing this plant? _____

_____

What parts of the plant did I eat (if edible)? *(e.g. root, leaf, fruit, flower):* _____

_____

If I didn't eat the plant, what did I do with it? *(e.g. made flower bouquets or I liked growing it for fun):*

_____

Would I grow this plant again? If not why?

Picture of Plant

Year _____

Plant: _____

Grown in: _____

Container: _____ Raised Bed: _____

Ground: _____

Planted Where?

Full Sun: _____ Shade: _____

Part Sun /Part Shade: _____

Did I start this plant from seed? _____

Date started seedlings: _____

Date I direct seeded: _____

I bought this plant: _____

Date planted: _____

How many planted: _____

Date harvested: _____

What was my yield for this plant(s)?

_____

Growing Notes
Suggested questions: How well did this plant grow? Any problem(s) growing this plant? If so, how did I fix it? How often did I have to water and was it enough?

My Garden Journal

Harvesting Notes

Suggested questions: What did the product look like? Did I grow too much or too little? Was there enough product to feed me? What was the color, smell, taste? Did I like it? Did it meet my expectations?

Plant

_____

_____

Soil Amendments Used

Before Planting: _____ During Growing Season: _____

After Harvesting: _____
(i.e. commercial compost; homemade compost; worm castings; compost tea)

What type of soil did this plant grow in?   Loam: _____   Clay Soil: _____

        Commercial Potting Soil: _____   Sandy Loam: _____   Don't know: _____

I purchased this seed or plant from: _____

                                                 Was it Organic?: _____ or Non-organic?:_____

What was my purpose for growing this plant? _____

_____

What parts of the plant did I eat (if edible)? *(e.g. root, leaf, fruit, flower):* _____

_____

If I didn't eat the plant, what did I do with it? *(e.g. made flower bouquets or I liked growing it for fun):*

_____

Would I grow this plant again? If not why?

My Garden Journal

Picture of Plant

Year _____

Plant: _____

Grown in: _____

Container: _____ Raised Bed: _____

Ground: _____

Planted Where?

Full Sun: _____ Shade: _____

Part Sun /Part Shade: _____

Did I start this plant from seed? _____

Date started seedlings: _____

Date I direct seeded: _____

I bought this plant: _____

Date planted: _____

How many planted: _____

Date harvested: _____

What was my yield for this plant(s)?

_____

Growing Notes
Suggested questions: How well did this plant grow? Any problem(s) growing this plant? If so, how did I fix it? How often did I have to water and was it enough?

My Garden Journal

Harvesting Notes

Suggested questions: What did the product look like? Did I grow too much or too little? Was there enough product to feed me? What was the color, smell, taste? Did I like it? Did it meet my expectations?

Plant _____

_____

Soil Amendments Used

Before Planting: _____ During Growing Season: _____

After Harvesting: _____
(i.e. commercial compost; homemade compost; worm castings; compost tea)

What type of soil did this plant grow in?   Loam: _____   Clay Soil: _____

        Commercial Potting Soil: _____   Sandy Loam: _____   Don't know: _____

I purchased this seed or plant from: _____

Was it Organic?: _____ or Non-organic?: _____

What was my purpose for growing this plant? _____

_____

What parts of the plant did I eat (if edible)? *(e.g. root, leaf, fruit, flower)*: _____

_____

If I didn't eat the plant, what did I do with it? *(e.g. made flower bouquets or I liked growing it for fun)*:

_____

Would I grow this plant again? If not why?

Picture of Plant

Year _____

Plant: _____

Grown in: _____

Container: _____ Raised Bed: _____

Ground: _____

Planted Where?

Full Sun: _____ Shade: _____

Part Sun /Part Shade: _____

Did I start this plant from seed? _____

Date started seedlings: _____

Date I direct seeded: _____

I bought this plant: _____

Date planted: _____

How many planted: _____

Date harvested: _____

What was my yield for this plant(s)?

_____

Growing Notes
Suggested questions: How well did this plant grow? Any problem(s) growing this plant? If so, how did I fix it? How often did I have to water and was it enough?

My Garden Journal

Harvesting Notes

Suggested questions: What did the product look like? Did I grow too much or too little? Was there enough product to feed me? What was the color, smell, taste? Did I like it? Did it meet my expectations?

Plant

_____

_____

Soil Amendments Used

Before Planting: _____ During Growing Season: _____

After Harvesting: _____
(i.e. commercial compost; homemade compost; worm castings; compost tea)

What type of soil did this plant grow in?   Loam: _____   Clay Soil: _____

        Commercial Potting Soil: _____   Sandy Loam: _____   Don't know: _____

I purchased this seed or plant from: _____

Was it Organic?: _____ or Non-organic?: _____

What was my purpose for growing this plant? _____

_____

What parts of the plant did I eat (if edible)? *(e.g. root, leaf, fruit, flower):* _____

_____

If I didn't eat the plant, what did I do with it? *(e.g. made flower bouquets or I liked growing it for fun):*

_____

Would I grow this plant again? If not why?

My Garden Journal

Picture of Plant

Year _____

Plant: _____

Grown in: _____

Container: _____ Raised Bed: _____

Ground: _____

Planted Where?

Full Sun: _____ Shade: _____

Part Sun /Part Shade: _____

Did I start this plant from seed? _____

Date started seedlings: _____

Date I direct seeded: _____

I bought this plant: _____

Date planted: _____

How many planted: _____

Date harvested: _____

What was my yield for this plant(s)?

_____

Growing Notes
Suggested questions: How well did this plant grow? Any problem(s) growing this plant? If so, how did I fix it? How often did I have to water and was it enough?

My Garden Journal

Harvesting Notes

Suggested questions: What did the product look like? Did I grow too much or too little? Was there enough product to feed me? What was the color, smell, taste? Did I like it? Did it meet my expectations?

Plant

_____

Soil Amendments Used

Before Planting: _____ During Growing Season: _____

After Harvesting: _____
(i.e. commercial compost; homemade compost; worm castings; compost tea)

What type of soil did this plant grow in?   Loam: _____   Clay Soil: _____

    Commercial Potting Soil: _____   Sandy Loam: _____   Don't know: _____

I purchased this seed or plant from: _____

    Was it Organic?: _____ or Non-organic?: _____

What was my purpose for growing this plant? _____

_____

What parts of the plant did I eat (if edible)? *(e.g. root, leaf, fruit, flower)*: _____

_____

If I didn't eat the plant, what did I do with it? *(e.g. made flower bouquets or I liked growing it for fun)*:

_____

Would I grow this plant again? If not why?

My Garden Journal

Picture of Plant

Year _____

Plant: _____

Grown in: _____

Container: _____ Raised Bed: _____

Ground: _____

Planted Where?

Full Sun: _____ Shade: _____

Part Sun /Part Shade: _____

Did I start this plant from seed? _____

Date started seedlings: _____

Date I direct seeded: _____

I bought this plant: _____

Date planted: _____

How many planted: _____

Date harvested: _____

What was my yield for this plant(s)?

_____

_____

Growing Notes
Suggested questions: How well did this plant grow? Any problem(s) growing this plant? If so, how did I fix it? How often did I have to water and was it enough?

Harvesting Notes

Suggested questions: What did the product look like? Did I grow too much or too little? Was there enough product to feed me? What was the color, smell, taste? Did I like it? Did it meet my expectations?

Plant _____

Soil Amendments Used

Before Planting: _____ During Growing Season: _____

After Harvesting: _____
(i.e. commercial compost; homemade compost; worm castings; compost tea)

What type of soil did this plant grow in? Loam: _____ Clay Soil: _____

Commercial Potting Soil: _____ Sandy Loam: _____ Don't know: _____

I purchased this seed or plant from: _____

Was it Organic?: _____ or Non-organic?: _____

What was my purpose for growing this plant? _____
_____

What parts of the plant did I eat (if edible)? *(e.g. root, leaf, fruit, flower)*: _____
_____

If I didn't eat the plant, what did I do with it? *(e.g. made flower bouquets or I liked growing it for fun)*:
_____

Would I grow this plant again? If not why?

My Garden Journal

Picture of Plant

Year_____

Plant: _____

Grown in:_____

Container: _____ Raised Bed: _____

Ground: _____

Planted Where?

Full Sun: _____ Shade: _____

Part Sun /Part Shade: _____

Did I start this plant from seed?_____

Date started seedlings: _____

Date I direct seeded: _____

I bought this plant: _____

Date planted: _____

How many planted: _____

Date harvested: _____

What was my yield for this plant(s)?

_____

Growing Notes

Suggested questions: How well did this plant grow? Any problem(s) growing this plant? If so, how did I fix it? How often did I have to water and was it enough?

Harvesting Notes

Suggested questions: What did the product look like? Did I grow too much or too little? Was there enough product to feed me? What was the color, smell, taste? Did I like it? Did it meet my expectations?

Plant

_____

Soil Amendments Used

Before Planting: _____ During Growing Season: _____

After Harvesting: _____

(i.e. commercial compost; homemade compost; worm castings; compost tea)

What type of soil did this plant grow in?　　　　　Loam: _____　　　Clay Soil: _____

　　　　Commercial Potting Soil: _____　　Sandy Loam: _____　　Don't know: _____

I purchased this seed or plant from: _____

　　　　　　　　　　　　　　　　　Was it Organic?: _____ or Non-organic?: _____

What was my purpose for growing this plant? _____

_____

What parts of the plant did I eat (if edible)? *(e.g. root, leaf, fruit, flower)*: _____

_____

If I didn't eat the plant, what did I do with it? *(e.g. made flower bouquets or I liked growing it for fun)*:

_____

Would I grow this plant again? If not why?

Picture of Plant

Year _____

Plant: _____

Grown in: _____

Container: _____ Raised Bed: _____

Ground: _____

Planted Where?

Full Sun: _____ Shade: _____

Part Sun /Part Shade: _____

Did I start this plant from seed? _____

Date started seedlings: _____

Date I direct seeded: _____

I bought this plant: _____

Date planted: _____

How many planted: _____

Date harvested: _____

What was my yield for this plant(s)?

_____

Growing Notes

Suggested questions: How well did this plant grow? Any problem(s) growing this plant? If so, how did I fix it? How often did I have to water and was it enough?

My Garden Journal

Harvesting Notes

Suggested questions: What did the product look like? Did I grow too much or too little? Was there enough product to feed me? What was the color, smell, taste? Did I like it? Did it meet my expectations?

Plant

_____

Soil Amendments Used

Before Planting: _____ During Growing Season: _____

After Harvesting: _____

(i.e. commercial compost; homemade compost; worm castings; compost tea)

What type of soil did this plant grow in?   Loam: _____   Clay Soil: _____

        Commercial Potting Soil: _____   Sandy Loam: _____   Don't know: _____

I purchased this seed or plant from: _____

Was it Organic?: _____ or Non-organic?: _____

What was my purpose for growing this plant? _____

_____

What parts of the plant did I eat (if edible)? *(e.g. root, leaf, fruit, flower):* _____

_____

If I didn't eat the plant, what did I do with it? *(e.g. made flower bouquets or I liked growing it for fun):*

_____

Would I grow this plant again? If not why?

© 2020 All Rights Reserved Brenda J. Sullivan, Thompson Street Farm LLC

Picture of Plant

Year _____

Plant: _____

Grown in: _____

Container: _____ Raised Bed: _____

Ground: _____

Planted Where?

Full Sun: _____ Shade: _____

Part Sun /Part Shade: _____

Did I start this plant from seed? _____

Date started seedlings: _____

Date I direct seeded: _____

I bought this plant: _____

Date planted: _____

How many planted: _____

Date harvested: _____

What was my yield for this plant(s)?

_____

Growing Notes

Suggested questions: How well did this plant grow? Any problem(s) growing this plant? If so, how did I fix it?
How often did I have to water and was it enough?

Harvesting Notes

Suggested questions: What did the product look like? Did I grow too much or too little? Was there enough product to feed me? What was the color, smell, taste? Did I like it? Did it meet my expectations?

Plant

_____

_____

Soil Amendments Used

Before Planting: _____ During Growing Season: _____

After Harvesting: _____

(i.e. commercial compost; homemade compost; worm castings; compost tea)

What type of soil did this plant grow in?   Loam: _____   Clay Soil: _____

    Commercial Potting Soil: _____   Sandy Loam: _____   Don't know: _____

I purchased this seed or plant from: _____

Was it Organic?: _____ or Non-organic?: _____

What was my purpose for growing this plant? _____

_____

What parts of the plant did I eat (if edible)? *(e.g. root, leaf, fruit, flower)*: _____

_____

If I didn't eat the plant, what did I do with it? *(e.g. made flower bouquets or I liked growing it for fun)*:

_____

Would I grow this plant again? If not why?

Picture of Plant

Year _____

Plant: _____

Grown in: _____

Container: _____ Raised Bed: _____

Ground: _____

Planted Where?

Full Sun: _____ Shade: _____

Part Sun /Part Shade: _____

Did I start this plant from seed? _____

Date started seedlings: _____

Date I direct seeded: _____

I bought this plant: _____

Date planted: _____

How many planted: _____

Date harvested: _____

What was my yield for this plant(s)?

_____

Growing Notes

Suggested questions: How well did this plant grow? Any problem(s) growing this plant? If so, how did I fix it? How often did I have to water and was it enough?

My Garden Journal

Harvesting Notes

Suggested questions: What did the product look like? Did I grow too much or too little? Was there enough product to feed me? What was the color, smell, taste? Did I like it? Did it meet my expectations?

Plant _____

_____

Soil Amendments Used

Before Planting: _____ During Growing Season: _____

After Harvesting: _____
(i.e. commercial compost; homemade compost; worm castings; compost tea)

What type of soil did this plant grow in? Loam: _____ Clay Soil: _____

Commercial Potting Soil: _____ Sandy Loam: _____ Don't know: _____

I purchased this seed or plant from: _____

Was it Organic?: _____ or Non-organic?: _____

What was my purpose for growing this plant? _____

_____

What parts of the plant did I eat (if edible)? *(e.g. root, leaf, fruit, flower)*: _____

_____

If I didn't eat the plant, what did I do with it? *(e.g. made flower bouquets or I liked growing it for fun)*:

_____

Would I grow this plant again? If not why?

© 2020 All Rights Reserved Brenda J. Sullivan, Thompson Street Farm LLC

Picture of Plant

Year _____

Plant: _____

Grown in: _____

Container: _____ Raised Bed: _____

Ground: _____

Planted Where?

Full Sun: _____ Shade: _____

Part Sun /Part Shade: _____

Did I start this plant from seed? _____

Date started seedlings: _____

Date I direct seeded: _____

I bought this plant: _____

Date planted: _____

How many planted: _____

Date harvested: _____

What was my yield for this plant(s)?

_____

Growing Notes
Suggested questions: How well did this plant grow? Any problem(s) growing this plant? If so, how did I fix it?
How often did I have to water and was it enough?

My Garden Journal

Harvesting Notes

Suggested questions: What did the product look like? Did I grow too much or too little? Was there enough product to feed me? What was the color, smell, taste? Did I like it? Did it meet my expectations?

Plant
_____

_____

Soil Amendments Used

Before Planting: _____ During Growing Season: _____

After Harvesting: _____
(i.e. commercial compost; homemade compost; worm castings; compost tea)

What type of soil did this plant grow in?   Loam: _____   Clay Soil: _____

     Commercial Potting Soil: _____   Sandy Loam: _____   Don't know: _____

I purchased this seed or plant from: _____

Was it Organic?: _____ or Non-organic?: _____

What was my purpose for growing this plant? _____

_____

What parts of the plant did I eat (if edible)? *(e.g. root, leaf, fruit, flower)*: _____

_____

If I didn't eat the plant, what did I do with it? *(e.g. made flower bouquets or I liked growing it for fun)*:

_____

Would I grow this plant again? If not why?

Resources

Seeds, Plants, Tubers Resources

(I recommend the seed and products from the following companies as being top quality based on my use over many years.)

Baker Creek Heirloom and Rare Seeds: Organic and nonorganic rare vegetable and flower seeds. www.rareseeds.com

Fedco Co-op: Organic seeds, tubers, nut trees, gardening supplies, and instruction videos. www.fedcoseeds.com

Field and Forest Products: Organic indoor and outdoor mushroom kits and mushroom growing supplies. www.fieldforest.net

Johnny's Selected Seeds: Organic seeds, gardening supplies, and instruction videos. www.johnnyseeds.com

Kitazawa Seed Company: Organic and nonorganic Asian Seeds. www.kitazawaseed.com

Peaceful Valley Farm Supply: Organic seeds, plants, nut trees, fruit bushes and vines, tubers, gardening supplies, and instruction videos. www.groworganic.com

Sprout People: Organic and nonorganic seeds for microgreens and sprouts. https://sproutpeople.org

Territorial Seed Company: Organic seeds, plants, nut trees, fruit bushes and vines, tubers, gardening supplies. www.territorialseed.com

Natural Fertilizer Suppliers:

Neptunes Harvest Organic Fertilizers: Liquid hydrolyzed fish and seeded fertilizers. www.neptunesharvest.com

Gardening and Other Books

I highly recommend the following books, which I own and refer to time and time again.

100 Plants to Feed Bees: Provide a Healthy Habitat to Help Pollinators Thrive. By The Xerces Society

All New Square Foot Gardening, 3rd Edition. By Mel Bartholomew

Indoor Kitchen Gardening: Turn Your Home into a Year-Round Vegetable Garden. By Elizabeth Millard

The Bee: A Natural History. By Noah Willson-Rich

The Urban Bounty: How to Grow Fresh Food Anywhere. By Allison Houghton

The Winter Harvest Handbook: Year Round Vegetable Production Using Deep-Organic Vegetable Techniques and Unheated Greenhouses. By Eliot Colman

Worms Eat My Garbage: How to Set Up and Maintain a Worm Composting System. By Mary Appelhof

Seed Saver and International Seed Vault Resources

Seed Savers Exchange Heirloom Seeds: A seed exchange nonprofit that encourages the collecting and exchanging of seeds for the home gardener within the United States. To find a depository near you, go to their website.
www.seedsavers.org

Svalbard Global Seed Vault: Learn about scientists from around the world collecting seeds to save for the future. The Svalbard seed vault, located in Norway, is part of the Global Diversity Crop Trust.

In many regions in the world, plants are extinct due to a variety of reasons. Wars, drought, floods, and human destruction are some of the reasons. The mission of these vaults is to collect and store seeds from every region on the planet, so when the conditions are favorable again, native plants can be reintroduced to their home region.

www.croptrust.org/our-work/svalbard-global-seed-vault/International Seed Vault

Other Websites

Discover Life (International): This organization's mission: "...to assemble and share knowledge in order to improve education, health, agriculture, economic development, and conservation throughout the world."

This website offers tools to study natural history and the effects of the changing climate. It has links to species maps in various countries (Global Mapper) and has North American identification guides.
www.discoverlife.org

The National Audubon Society (USA): This is an organization that dedicates itself to protecting birds and their habitats. There are many Audubon educational centers around the US. To find out where the nearest center near you check out their website.
www.audubon.org

National Butterfly Center: The National Butterfly Center is a project of the North American Butterfly Association (NABA),

a nonprofit organization dedicated to the conservation and study of wild butterflies in their native habitats.
www.nationalbutterflycenter.org

National Honey Board (USA): Learn about honey and how bees make it.
www.honey.com

U.S. Plant Zone Map: USDA Department of Agriculture Plant Hardiness Zone Map.
https://planthardiness.ars.usda.gov/PHZMWeb/

Xerces Society: This is an international nonprofit that protects the natural world through the conservation of invertebrates (e.g., Monarch Butterfly) and their habit
https

Notes

_____

_____

_____

_____

_____

_____

_____

_____

_____

_____

_____

_____

_____

_____

About The Sullivan Family

Brenda Sullivan lives in South Glastonbury, Connecticut with her husband Paul and their daughter Katie.

They are avid nature lovers who took their love of gardening to a new level by converting their small property into a micro farm called Thompson Street Farm LLC.

Brenda is an herbalist and market gardener who specializes in growing lavender, medicinal herbs, and flowers. She also makes handcrafted goat's milk herbal soaps and herbal bath products using the herbs, flowers, fruits, and vegetables grown on their farm or purchased from other local farmers.

Katie, the love of their life and the center of their universe, has severe cerebral palsy, epilepsy, is legally blind (with limited vision), and has other serious medical conditions. Although Katie is nonverbal and wheelchair-bound, these challenges haven't prevented her from experiencing life.

Katie experiences her world on her terms. With the help of assistive technology, other sensory adaptations, and years of homeschooling experience, Katie understands basic concepts and has developed many interests. These include an appreciation for music, painting with her mother and listening to stories.

She loves being outdoors, and we've discovered that enabling her to experience her natural world has been Katie's best educator. This has been our inspiration for creating nature-themed children's books.

Other Books by Brenda J. Sullivan

Journals

This journal has 22 beaufitful color pictures of lavender and the wildlife living in our garden.

This journal has beautiful black and white lavender illustrations on all the journal pages.

To learn more about our books or join our newsletter go to
www.brendajsullivanbooks.com

Connect with Brenda Online

www.brendajsullivanbooks.com
www.thompsonstreetfarm.com
www.farmtobath.com
www.livingandlovinherbs.com

Brenda J. Sullivan

Kids Count Series

Nature Themed Early Reader and Coloring Book

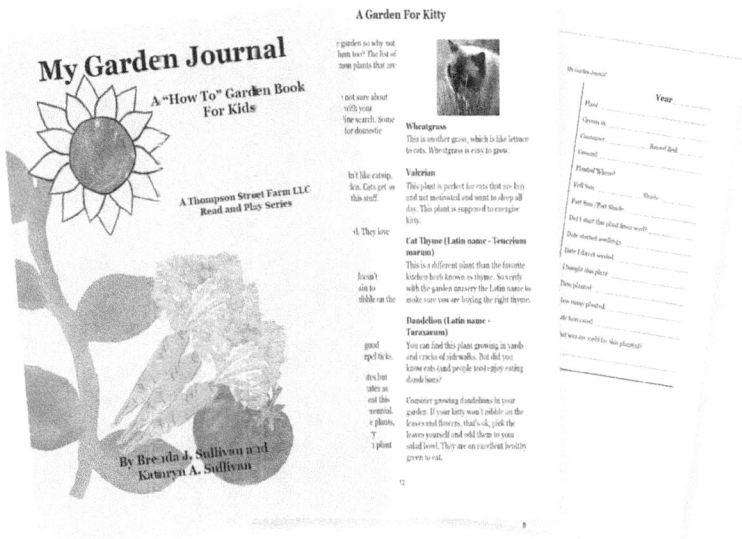

Available online and in all book retailers
Just ask them to order

www.ingramcontent.com/pod-product-compliance
Lightning Source LLC
Chambersburg PA
CBHW081116080526
44587CB00021B/3616